J

RAF AIRCRAFT TODAY: 1

PHANTOM

RAF AIRCRAFT TODAY: 1

PHANTOM

Bill Gunston

LONDON
IAN ALLAN LTD

CONTENTS

	Introduction	5
1	The British Phantoms	6
2	With the Royal Navy	14
3	RAF Strike Command: Attack/ Reconnaissance	32
4	RAF Strike Command: Air Defence	44
5	RAF Germany: Attack/ Reconnaissance	64
6	RAF Germany: Air Defence	76
7	RAF Phantoms Today	88
	Appendices	
1	Basic Specifications	95
2	Aircraft Built	96

Cover:
RAF Phantom FRG2 XV412 of No 29 Squadron pictured during a sortie over the North Sea in March 1984.
Denis J. Calvert

First published 1984

ISBN 0 7110 1383 7

Published by Ian Allan Ltd, Shepperton, Surrey; and printed by Ian Allan Printing Ltd at their works at Coombelands in Runnymede, England.

INTRODUCTION

Seven years ago Ian Allan was kind enough to ask me to lead off a new series of Modern Combat Aircraft with a book on the F-4 Phantom. Even at that time the Phantom was already a legend. Today it is longer in the tooth, but it still happens to be the only 'fighter' in the Royal Air Force, and Ian Allan had no doubt whatever that it should be the subject of the first of another new series dealing with the aircraft of the RAF.

Apart from the fact that they both deal with the same basic type of aircraft, there is no overlap at all between these two books. To a considerable degree the story of the British Phantoms is a totally different story from that of the F-4 variants flown by US services and other export customers. Right at the start the British bought the Phantom to fly from aircraft carriers which were too small for a Phantom without fairly extensive modification to the aircraft. It is only natural that British avionics and other equipment should have been preferred, and that British aircraft firms should have shared in licence manufacture of parts of the airframe.

What was less obvious was the decision to change to a British engine. Rolls-Royce had an excellent engine, which appeared to offer the prospect of a generally enhanced performance, but in fact the switch in propulsion system proved a great disappointment which not only grossly inflated the price but in some respects actually degraded the performance. Despite this, the British Phantoms have always been splendid aircraft. They have been flown by the Royal Navy and RAF in many parts of the world, including today the remote Falkland Islands.

We should not forget that from April 1957 until well into the 1960s the official British view at the political level was that manned fighters were obsolete, and that it was folly to waste public funds on their purchase or improvement. The link between this policy and the Phantom was an all-British fighter which could take off vertically, and which met a NATO requirement for a V/STOL tactical aircraft with supersonic performance. From more than 20 years on, it is hard to say whether ditching this versatile new-technology British aircraft and instead buying an American long-runway fighter was a wise decision.

Predictably, the Anglicised Phantom has served Britain well. Many people will be delighted to see this book, which pays tribute to one of the greatest military aircraft of modern times.

The author would like to thank several enthusiasts for the loan of photographs, including Martin Horseman and, especially Robert F. Dorr who also provided the F-4J information in an appendix.

Bill Gunston
Haslemere,
England,
1984

1
THE BRITISH PHANTOMS

Below:
Though it had actually flown for the first time on the previous day, this photograph of the first British Phantom was taken on 28 June 1966, on the occasion of its first 'official' flight during Anglo/US ceremonies at Lambert St Louis airport. This first flight came precisely a month after the first flight of the F-4J, the US Navy model on which the F-4K was based.
MCAIR via R. F. Dorr

The prototype Phantom (strictly, the Phantom II), then called the F4H-1, made its maiden flight from Lambert-St Louis airport adjacent to the growing factory of MCAIR (McDonnell Aircraft) on 27 May 1958. Hardly beautiful, it was at least distinctive, with a very broad wing of almost 45° delta shape, with extended dogtooth outer wings sharply dihedralled upwards, in contrast to the sharply downsloping slab tailplanes. The vertical tail was remarkably broad and squat, engine bleed air was blown at supersonic speed from slits along the drooping leading-edge flaps and broad but short-span trailing-edge flaps, and lateral control was effected by quite small ailerons between the flaps and the hinges of the folding outer wings, in partnership with small spoilers just upstream of them. There were two Martin-Baker H5 seats in tandem, and a unique feature was that under the fuselage, made exceptionally broad by the large lateral inlet ducts, were recesses for four Sparrow AAMs. No gun was fitted, but there was potential, at that time unrealised, for a tremendous external load of many types of store.

The production F-4B of the US Navy and Marines quickly became the standard against which other fighters of the early 1960s were judged, though it was still a surprise when a minimum-change F-4C model was adopted by, of all people, the rival USAF. It is much less surprising that covetous eyes were cast on the Phantom by the Royal Navy, which never wholly liked the idea of a vectored-thrust V/STOL originally planned for the RAF. The RAF wished to replace the Hunter in the land-based fighter, attack and reconnaissance roles, and in retrospect it is perhaps unfortunate that it was just at this time, in 1962, that the Pentagon was buzzing with the idea of 'commonality' in fighter procurement between air force and navy, with the notorious TFX (later F-111) programme. It seemed logical to develop a variant of the RAF's Hawker P1154 to meet the Royal Navy's parallel need for a replacement for the Sea Vixen interceptor and Scimitar strike aircraft.

The P1154 presented severe technical and operational challenges, but with good will and a wish to achieve success, rather than a wish to achieve failure, P1154 versions could have become standard equipment in both UK flying services by about 1968-9. As it was, the 'dark blues' were only too eager to stick rigidly to rules and newly invented requirements which history was to show were unnecessary, but which were enough to bring the P1154RN to a grinding halt. Chief among these was a demand for two engines, which for a vectored-thrust STOVL aircraft is hard to justify; another was two cockpits, while Harrier-style landing gear was rejected as incompatible with carrier operation. Increasingly the Royal Navy, most ably led by the Chief of Defence Staff, Lord Louis Mountbatten, campaigned for the American Phantom. Had the Senior Service never been involved, the P1154 would have moved much faster and more surely. As it was, the demon of commonality held the programme back so that, when the Navy finally pulled out in February 1964, no standard of design had even been agreed.

Immediately, on 27 February, the Minister of Defence, Peter Thorneycroft, announced that the replacement for the Sea Vixen would be the Phantom. It was planned to buy 140 direct from McDonnell, the first 60 being priced at £45million (in view of the price of today's Hornet and Mirage 2000 it is worth emphasising that this was the bill for all 60). It was obvious that Britain would seek some kind of industrial offset or manufacturing participation, and though the immediate target was the avionic fit of 'black boxes' a much bigger possibility for British participation was the engine.

Rolls-Royce had been forced to abandon the powerful RB141 Medway turbofan by BEA's decision to scale down the DH121 Trident, and the resulting RB163 Spey was sized to below 10,000lb thrust. Its small size, however, made it suitable as a replacement for such US straight jet engines as the J57 and J79, and an afterburner could double its thrust, so the great Derby company lost no time trying to get into a US combat-aircraft programme. It tried especially hard with the Phantom, and in February 1962 McDonnell teamed with Rolls to make formal proposals for the F4H-2 for the Navy and F-110B for the USAF, in each case with an afterburning Spey engine. The Rolls engine promised to increase total thrust at takeoff from 34,000lb to a lusty 41,030lb, and also appeared on paper to offer greatly improved climb, ceiling, supersonic acceleration and combat radius or range. The Spey-Phantom looked impressive, but in 1962 it appeared a previous-generation aircraft; the US customers were polarised on the scintillating TFX.

Rolls then turned to the situation at home. It played a major part in undermining the P1154 programme as soon as it had become clear that the company's efforts to get a twin-Spey version accepted would not be successful. Once Rolls and the Mountbatten faction had got the Phantom substituted, there was no way the British government could really avoid agreeing to the existing engine, the General Electric J79, being replaced by the Spey. McDonnell dusted off the 1962 installation drawings, and by March 1964 a team from Derby was at St Louis doing the detail engineering. It was a major redesign, because compared with the J79 the Spey was shorter, fractionally heavier and not only

Right:
The extra-extensible nose gear shows clearly on XT598, the fourth Phantom on British account, as MCAIR employees re-check one of its unfamiliar engines. The engines were rolled in on the same old dollies used for J79s, but with an added steel-tube truss picking up the Spey mounts. *MCAIR*

much more powerful (at low airspeeds) but gulped air at the rate of 208lb/sec compared with 169. The entire engine bay had to be redesigned, the inlet bellmouths and ducts increased in width by some 6in, the rear 'boat-tails' aft of the much larger nozzles reprofiled and, because though cooler the jets from the engines were closer to the structure, much of the rear fuselage was changed from aluminium to titanium.

Designing this installation took most of 1964-5, by which time the new baseline US Navy aircraft, the F-4J, had completed its design and begun to replace the B on the St Louis line. This was made the basis for the British F-4K, and the same Westinghouse AWG-10 pulse-doppler radar was used, more powerful than that of the F-4B and with look-down capability. To meet the severe overall length limitation of 54ft imposed by Royal Navy carriers the entire radar aerial and radome was arranged to hinge round through 180°. To allow full-weight takeoffs to be made on *Ark Royal's* catapults, less powerful than those of US carriers and unable to give the same WOD (wind over deck) speed, the nose leg was made extra-extensible (to a remarkable full extension of 40in, 1.03m) giving such a nose-up angle that WOD requirement was reduced by 11kt (20km/h). For the same reason the lift after a cat shot was increased by fitting larger flaps, drooping ailerons, and tailplanes with inverted slats on the leading edge, all these improvements being at once also incorporated in the F-4J. To permit carrier landings at 24ft/sec vertical velocity at the increased weight of 38,000lb (17,237kg) the stronger main gears and larger tyres of the F-4J were chosen, as well as a stronger arrester hook not used on the US aircraft. The final significant changes were the addition of auxiliary doors on each side above the afterburners to discharge turbine-cooling and bleed air at low airspeeds or on the ground, an all-British suite of nav/com avionics, and extensive revision to cockpit instrumentation.

In October 1964 Britain had elected a Labour government which announced that the British aircraft industry was 'grossly undesirable' and that it was 'far preferable to buy cheaper planes from the USA'. On 2 February 1965 the P1154 for the RAF was cancelled, but in this case the main reason given was one of timing. Prime Minister Wilson said 'it would not have been in service in time to serve as a Hunter replacement'. Defence Minister Healey at once announced that the RAF, like the RN, would instead receive the Phantom, and thus 'will get its Hunter replacement four years earlier'. There is no point in flogging horses long dead, but the fact remains that the Hunters were not 'almost falling apart', as they were described in 1965, and in fact continued flying with the RN and RAF (and many other nations) in 1984. Neither did buying the Phantom produce a replacement any sooner, and it certainly did not result in a reduced price, though it

Above:
This photograph was taken at Boscombe Down for ML Aviation, who are demonstrating their new model of aircraft handler. Fixed to it is XT598, second pre-production F-4K, with a camera on a special pylon at the right wingtip to record separation of the black/white dummy nuclear store on the centreline. *MoD via ML*

could be claimed that the P1154 price might have risen between 1965 and 1968. What really was significant was that it eliminated the option of a V/STOL aircraft and instead kept the RAF, like other air forces, based on giant airfields whose precise locations are known and which happen to be available in only a very few places (and none within 3,500 miles of the Falklands, for example).

The only positive thing switching to the Phantom did appear to offer was to eliminate technical risk. The plan was to rush through the conversion to the British engine and then deliver a total of 290, of which the second batch of 150 would go to the RAF. It did not turn out like this at all. The new government disliked not only the home aircraft industry but also the Fleet Air Arm, and soon announced that the new carrier, CV-01, would be cancelled and that when she came to require a major refit *Ark Royal* would be withdrawn, bringing to an end fixed-wing aviation in the RN. Thus it was decided that, far from receiving 140 Phantoms, only one RN first-line squadron would operate the type. As explained in the next chapter the F-4K, with British designation Phantom FG1, was severely curtailed — and almost half of those actually built went direct to the RAF.

As for the RAF, production authorisation for its F-4M was given on 5 May 1965, and the first contract was received by McDonnell the following month. This version was again modified, compared with the F-4K, though the engine installations were almost identical. The double-extension nose leg, catapult hooks, tailplane slats and aileron droop system were removed, but anti-skid brakes were added and complete revision took place of avionics. The radar fire-control was modified to AWG-12 standard, though designation is officially 11/12, with Ferranti of Edinburgh as chief UK contractor to the prime supplier Westinghouse. Ferranti also provided the completely new inertial nav/attack system. An HF com system was added, with shunt aerials in the sides of the fin (not the same as on American RF-4 reconnaissance Phantoms) and the associated boxes in the rear fuselage. VHF/UHF flush antennae were fitted in the fin cap (where RWR receivers went later, as noted in another chapter), ECM equipment and British IFF was provided for, and mounts and controls were added for a large strike camera to be clipped in at the rear of the forward left AAM recess. Provision was also made for various existing or planned RAF missiles, as well as the USAF's SUU-23 gun pod and a large multisensor reconnaissance pod, both carried on the centreline pylon.

The final task at management level was to find UK suppliers for airframe parts and equipment, though the shrinking size of the programme reduced total British content from the target of 50% to just under 45%. The principal airframe parts made in Britain were the outer wing, with droop flap, supplied by Shorts from Belfast, and the complete rear fuselage and tail, fixed inboard leading edges and six engine doors, all supplied by BAC from Preston. These were shipped to St Louis where the British Phantoms were assembled and flight tested. To support all British Phantoms in service, contracts were placed with Hawker Siddeley Aviation, which became McDonnell's 'sister company' with full design authority not only for major overhaul and repair but also for any modifications that might be necessary. In due course these contracts passed to British Aerospace Kingston-Brough Division, with all Phantom work centred at Brough, N Humberside, and the airfield at HOSM (Holme on Spalding Moor) which has now closed.

Above:
Taken in mid-1967 this photograph shows the first production F-4K, by this time called a Phantom FG1, over downtown St Louis on its first flight. It has MCAIR No 2097 at the top of the fin but still lacks the serial No XT857. This Phantom is today flying as aircraft 'C' of RAF 111 Squadron at Leuchars.
MCAIR via R. F. Dorr

Below:
Looking up at the cause of most of the drag trouble: XT860, the fourth production FG1, seen from a companion with 700P Sqn on early intensive trials. The huge Spey nozzles can be seen closed up in dry cruise. Between them is the massive pivot for the hook. Also visible are the airbrakes ahead of the flaps, the giant 500gal (600 US gal) centreline tank, a training Sidewinder and RN 2in rocket pod, and the fact that in those days the front Sparrow recesses were often left unballasted.
MoD

Above:
By the time they got to the RAF's version MCAIR had confidence and only two YF-4Ms were built prior to the main run. This was the first YF, pictured outside the plant before it was taken aloft by Joe Dobronski and Irv Burrows on 17 February 1967. *MCAIR via R. F. Dorr*

Below:
British Aerospace Kingston-Brough Division have from the start been foster parents to all British Phantoms, and have recently been involved in a major wing modification programme. Here the oldest of the current charges, XT598 (already pictured twice in this chapter), awaits its test crew at Holme on Spalding Moor after a complete major overhaul and updating. Today HOSM has closed. *BAe*

Above right:
XT597 is the first pre-production FG1, which has spent almost its entire life at the UK Aeroplane & Armament Experimental Establishment at Boscombe Down. Instead of bearing MoD(PE) colours it has a naval dark sea grey body and rudder with a red fin, and A&AEE written in white. The camera-packed tank is very non-standard. *AAEE via R. F. Dorr*

Right:
XV432 of No 6 Squadron. *MoD*

XT597

N

2

WITH THE ROYAL NAVY

Below:
XT859, the third production FG1, photographed at about 25,000ft on early intensive flying trials with No 700P Sqn, RN, from HMS *Heron*, RNAS Yeovilton. To extend mission endurance it has two 360gal wing tanks. *MoD (RN)*

A listing of numbers and serials of British Phantoms is provided in the Appendix. It will be seen that there were two YF-4K prototypes, followed by two pre-production aircraft which were intended to be to the standard of the Phantom FG1 for the Fleet Air Arm inventory, but in the event this was not possible. The first YF was very much an interim machine, but it did have the Rolls-Royce engines when it made its maiden flight at St Louis on 27 June 1966, precisely eight years and one month after the first flight of a Phantom on J79 engines from the same runway.

MCAIR pressed ahead with the F-4K and F-4M with all speed, but problems mounted. The most fundamental concerned propulsion. On the testbed the Spey 201, the engine fitted to prototype and early production British Phantoms, behaved perfectly. In the airframe it suffered from mismatching with the inlet system, and a more severe problem was that aerodynamic drag of the aircraft had been sharply increased by the changed fuselage shape, the increase being more than nine times that predicted. Much of the drag problem was traced to the base drag of the larger nozzles and reprofiled rear fuselage. Nothing could be done with the nozzles, but work went on at Derby, at Hucknall (the Rolls-Royce installation and flight-test establishment) and at St Louis for more than three years without ever resolving the difficulties.

Eventually two different marks of engine went into production for British Phantoms, the Mk 202 for the FGR2 for the RAF and the Mk 203, with special fast-lightup reheat augmentation (for carrier over-shoots) for the FG1. In the long term the cost was substantially increased, the published unit price to the Royal Navy rising by more than 500% — such politically contrived 'prices' are meaningless — and delivery was delayed until the first three FG1 aircraft were ferried by RN crews into RNAS Yeovilton (HMS *Heron*) on 25 April 1968.

By this time the planned termination of the RN fixed-wing force and withdrawal from East of Suez had slashed the RN Phantom force from 140 to only 28. The first five equipped 700P IFTU (Intensive Flying Trials Unit), formed at Yeovilton on 30 April 1968 and tasked with crew training and flogging the FG1 as hard as possible in simulated operational missions, which were primarily concerned with fleet defence and air interception. The first landing on a British carrier was on 2 June 1968 when a 700P crew arrived for trials aboard HMS *Eagle*. The full-scale flying training squadron, No 767, commissioned at Yeovilton on 14 January 1969, and trained all the air and ground crews to support Phantom operations by the Fleet Air Arm.

The sole operational unit, No 892 Sqn, was commissioned at Yeovilton on 1 March 1969, adopting the Greek letter omega as its emblem. Last of the alphabet, this character symbolised 892's role as the final fixed-wing squadron of the Fleet Air Arm — or so it was then thought. Standard finish of Royal Navy Phantoms was Dark Sea Grey (as stencilled on the aircraft) or Extra Dark Sea Grey (according to the Stores Ref for the paint) and white. All aircraft in the inventory were painted with a white three-figure individual number corresponding to the Modex numbers of the US Navy, together with a tail code: VL for RNAS Yeovilton, R for HMS *Ark Royal* or LU for RAF Leuchars.

No 892 could not help being an élite unit, though for most of its life the Royal Navy also had other fixed-wing squadrons flying Buccaneers and early-warning and COD (carrier on-board delivery)

Gannets. It embarked in *Ark Royal* for the first operational cruise, and sailed for Malta on 19 October 1970. This was also the first operational cruise of the stately *Ark* in her sixth Commission, following a major three-year refit in which she was given an $8\frac{1}{2}°$ angled deck, waist catapult and substantial topside strengthening to withstand the weight and jet blast of Phantoms. Now the famous ship is gone it seems churlish to recall that, at the time, there were many who wondered why the Phantoms of 892 Sqn were not being put aboard *Eagle*, which was better suited to them. Other members of the ship's Air Group comprised 809 Sqn Buccaneers, 824 Sqn Sea Kings, 859B Flight Gannet AEW3s and a Wessex SAR flight.

Throughout this commission, which ended in 1973, the Phantom performed admirably. For various reasons a substantial proportion of 892's aircrew were RAF. Contrary to plan no attempt was made to carry Martel or Bullpup missiles, and weapons were confined to GP bombs and standard RN 2in rockets (RAF rockets are usually the 68mm SNEB), with the occasional AIM-9B Sidewinder and other uncommon species. From Fort Lauderdale to Cyprus, and from Belize to Hamburg, and countless other places, 892 practised round-the-clock carrier operations, interceptions and the occasional bomb run on a splash target or other air/ground mission.

In 1975 the fin caps grew the ARI18228 passive receiver aerial fairing to give warning of illumination by hostile radars, giving the same change in shape as experienced by RAF Phantoms and, indeed, US Navy F-4Js. This occurred during *Ark's* 1974-6 cruise, which included visits to the USA in Bicentenary Year (1976), but it was on the 1978 and final cruise that several Phantoms visiting NAS Oceana were, secretly overnight, given US star insignia and with COLONIAL in place of the word ROYAL! By this time all active 892 aircraft had been painted in attractive nose insignia of red, white, blue, black and gold, originally to celebrate the Queen's Jubilee in 1977. In that year the nose emblem was a gold 77 topped by a crown, but in 1978 this was replaced by the squadron's own badge.

Apart from 892 the only RN Phantom unit in the late 1970s was the PTF (Phantom Training Flight), successor to 767 and located at RAF Leuchars. Always partly populated by 'light blue' personnel, PTF trained flight and ground crews for 892 until its sad final mission on 22 August 1977, the unit finally disbanding in May 1978. As for 892, the last cat shot from *Ark* was made by aircraft 012 (XT870), flown by Flt Lt Murdo MacLeod RAF, on 27 November 1978. This was only temporarily the end of RN high-speed aviation, because the first Sea Harrier had flown three months previously!

Below:
Two comparative views of some of the first FG1s to reach Britain. No 767 Sqn painted its stylised badge on the fin and a white three-digit number, corresponding to the US Navy Modex, mid-way along the fuselage (700P had a small Modex on the nose). Note also the tail code VL for Yeovilton. Unlike the RAF aircraft the FG1 has a prominent incidence scale so that the carrier crew chief could quickly verify the correct tailplane angle prior to cat release. Aircraft 155 (XT859) shows this scale with the tail at full negative incidence; No 150 (XT863) has the tail fully up, showing instead the fixed inverted slat. *IAL*

Below:
Two more comparative views of a 767 Sqn aircraft, in this case two different aspects of No 158 (XT866). In the takeoff the engines are in afterburner, and the nose gear is folding back after being in the normal (not doubly extended) position, which is adequate for takeoff from a runway. Blurred in the rear are a Chipmunk and Hunter T8. The landing picture shows the blown flaps and drooped ailerons in action. *IAL*

Above:
Shock diamonds glow as 767 Sqn's No 160 (XT876, last of the first batch) gets going for what the photographer called 'the best individual aerobatic flying seen for a long time. It terminated the routine by a high-speed sideways bunt, followed by a rocketing climb out of sight'. The occasion was Open Day at RAF Bentwaters. *Dennis Robinson*

Below:
Pair scramble by 767 Sqn aircraft in full afterburner (reheat), with everything out and drooped. Each aircraft has all four auxiliary air doors open, two beside the jetpipes and two under the wing, to expel engine bleed and admit cooling air. *MoD via IAL*

Below:
Two arrivals with the front-line unit, No 892 Sqn, replete with Omega tail emblem and the R tail letter denoting HMS *Ark Royal* (in earlier commissions the ship's letter had been O). Both aircraft (007 is XT871 and 013 is XV587) have the monster centreline tank, and 007 has twin stores carriers, with two rocket pods on the left wing. There are several reasons for folding wings on the ground. *IAL*

Below:
Another takeoff and landing comparison, this time with 892 Sqn aircraft whose Modex was painted on the nose. Fleet Air Arm aircraft do not carry a fin 'flash' unlike the RAF. In any case 892's fins were bright red. The side view clearly shows the angles of the flaps, ailerons and tailplanes, as well as the drooped leading edge; airbrakes remain closed. *IAL*

Top:
Arrival of an FG1 of 892 Sqn aboard USS *Independence* during cross-deck exercises in the Med. In the foreground are an F-4J and an RA-5C. As American F-4s are rare in this book, this is a good place to draw attention to the long fuel vent pipe projecting behind the tail, which makes most Phantoms roughly 6in longer than the British ones, whose pipe is cut off closer to the rudder. *MoD (RN)*

Above:
XV569 of POCU Training Flight photographed at Leuchars on 16 September 1972. Note absence of insignia other than the LU tail code. Parked behind is an FG1 of RAF No 43 Sqn.
Alan B. Carlaw

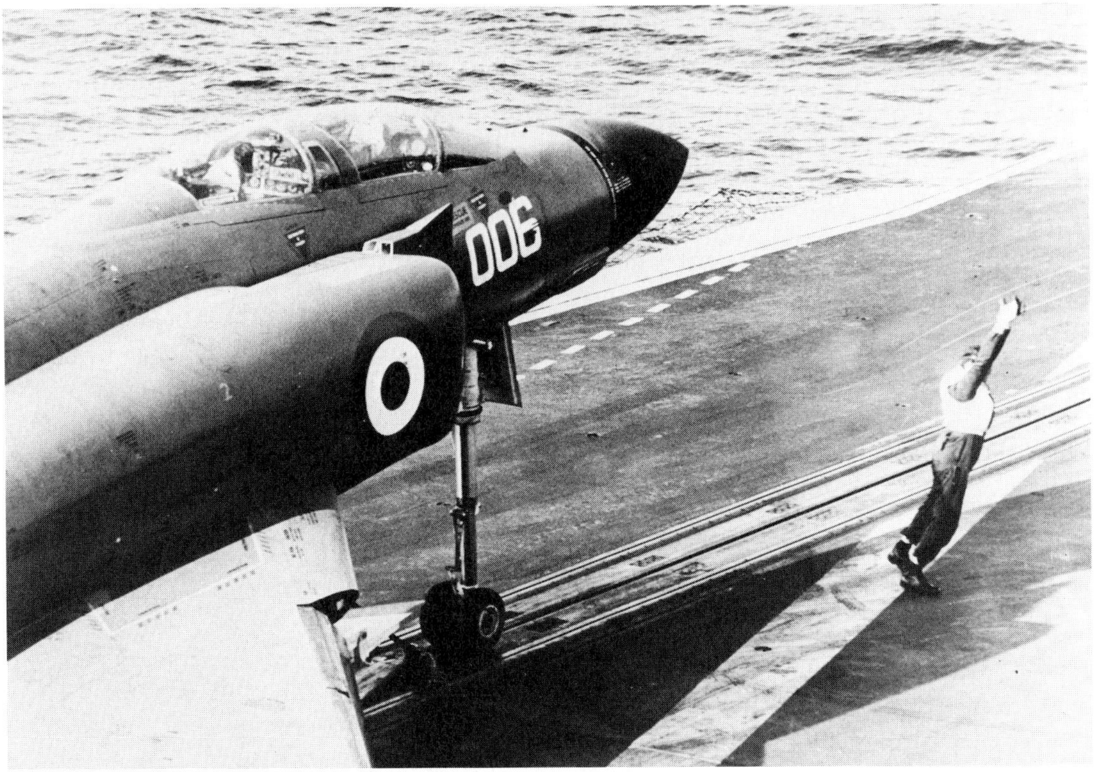

Above:
The 'Badger' gives thumbs up and No 006 is about to leave *Ark Royal* in what is called 'the longest three seconds in the world'. This view clearly shows the droop leading edge, long nose gear, inlet boundary-layer ejector nozzles and even the cockpits. *MoD (RN)*

Below:
FG1s of 892 Sqn parked outside squadron HQ at RAF Leuchars on 7 November 1972. Aircraft are 001 (XT870) and 003 (XV586). *Alan B. Carlaw*

Above:
Busy scene aboard *Ark Royal* in April 1975 during cross-deck exercises with visiting A-6s and F-4s (the latter from VF-33 and VF-102), from USS *Independence*. All the 892 Sqn Phantoms in the picture had fin-cap ECM aerials. *MoD(RN)*

Top right:
Just a year later and 892 Sqn put up two Phantoms to assist this gaggle which includes a Buccaneer from 809 Sqn, three A-7 Corsairs from VA-46 'The Clansmen' and a TA-4 from the Instrument Training School. All were flying from NAS Cecil Field, near Jacksonville, Florida, during an April 1976 visit of *Ark* to Mayport. *MoD (RN)*

Centre right:
One of *Ark's* Phantoms formates on an A-6E-15 from VA-176 (USS *America*) during NATO Southern Command exercise 'Display Determination' in the Mediterranean in October 1976. *MoD(RN)*

Right:
892 Sqn's No 005, flying from *Ark*, takes fuel from a KA-6D, with an escort of two F-4Js from Marine VMFA-333 'Shamrocks', all operating from the giant USS *Nimitz* during 'Display Determination' in October 1976. *MoD(RN)*

AB
NAVY
012
022

500
USS AMERICA
NAVY
VA-176
158533
AE
007
ROYAL NAVY

MARINES

002
01

ROYAL NAVY
002
012
011
007
005
004
003

Above left:
For Her Majesty's Silver Jubilee in 1977, No 892 Sqn painted every Phantom with this special insignia, red/white/blue stripes and a golden 77. The CO's aircraft (002) had a proper crown instead of just a coronet! *MoD(RN)*

Left:
892's complete line-up for the Silver Jubilee, on the apron at HMS *Heron*. One FG1 is awaiting its three-digit Modex and the one at the far end has recently changed its number which has both superimposed. *MoD(RN)*

Above:
The whole PTF (Phantom Training Flight) in formation for the first and last time on 22 August 1977; PTF provided crews for 892 Sqn and was disbanded in May 1978. The vic was led by Cdr Carl Davis, Senior Naval Officer at Leuchars, with his No 2 the Station Commander, Grp Capt Bill Maish. They were followed by Sqn Ldr Al Winkles, PTF CO, PTF staff crew and engineering officers, and a visiting 892 crew who joined for the ride. *RAF Leuchars*

Above:
The Jubilee markings stayed on 892's aircraft for the whole of Jubilee year, and this aircraft, XV589, was photographed during deck-landing practice aboard *Ark*. It looks immaculate. *MoD(RN)*

Below:
When Jubilee year was up, 892 did not like to erase the colourful markings so they replaced the 77 by a squadron badge. Here is 011 again, with training Sidewinders and four practice bombs, getting thumbs-up from the deck (cat) party and the flag up from the FDO (Flight Deck Officer) before being shot from the waist catapult, extra-extensible gear at full stretch. *MoD(RN)*

Right:
Two views of a launch of aircraft 014 from *Ark's* waist catapult in November 1978. Drill includes blown flaps fully down and ailerons drooped. *MoD(RN)*

R
ROYAL NAVY
014
14

R
ROYAL NAVY
XT863
014
14

Above:
An FG1 of Royal Navy No 892 Sqn lines up on the bow catapult of HMS *Ark Royal*, guided by the Flight Director. A training Sidewinder is under the starboard wing. *MoD(RN)*

Below:
Plenty of steam is escaping as an FG1 of 892 Sqn goes off the angled deck cat of *Ark Royal*, with the steel towing strop suddenly going slack. Four of the Royal Navy 36-tube 2in rocket launchers are carried. The Plane Guard Wessex is on station, and a Sea King HAS1 of 824 Sqn waits to recover. *MoD(RN)*

Top:
Engines almost at flight idling, two 892 Phantoms, (XV592, the last FG.1 built, and XV587) formate on the Fleet Air Arm Museum's Sea Fury, throttle almost firewalled and nose-down by comparison. *HMS Heron*

Above:
An F-4J from CVW-17 (USS *Forrestal*) shares *The Ark's* deck with Phantoms of 892 and Buccaneers of 809. Up for'ard, two AEW Gannets unfold ready for catapulting. *MoD(RN)*

3

RAF STRIKE COMMAND: ATTACK/ RECONNAISSANCE

Below:
Takeoff from Coningsby of XV432 of 6 Sqn for a photographic sortie. In the background can be seen most of the squadron and the Phantoms of 228 OCU. *MoD(RAF)*

The first Phantom to join the RAF was the very first production FGR2, XT891, which was ferried to Aldergrove (today Belfast airport) on 20 July 1968, and continued on 23 August to 228 OCU at Coningsby. This was only a few months earlier than the P1154 was to have been delivered, rather than Mr Healey's 'four years'; but at least, after the appalling government indecision and interference with the preceding British programme, the Phantom represented a solid hunk of metal with RAF roundels on it. Nobody appeared in the least concerned that by switching from the P1154 to the Phantom the RAF was nailing its flag very firmly to the US-led mast which said, in effect, 'We don't give a damn for Soviet missiles aimed at our airfields'.

From the start it was clear that the expected 'Super-Phantom' was not all it was cracked up to be. Indeed, four years later, when a senior RAF officer used those words to the author, he added 'And that's not meant to be a sick joke about the structural fatigue problem'. Like the F-111, which was a parallel programme in timing, the British Phantom seemed to run into every kind of intractable snag that it was possible to encounter.

Squadron pilots are not forever firewalling the throttles and trying to exceed Mach 2, and the fact that the Spey-Phantom was actually slower than Brand X was not immediately apparent, nor was it considered to imperil the kingdom. In any case the planned primary task of the FGR2 was to be close-support ground attack and reconnaissance, and this meant concentration on low-level operation. Here the worse transonic drag was of little consequence, whereas the good performance in cold power was judged a large plus. Specific range was found to be fractionally better than that of a USAF F-4, and acceleration and climb in maximum cold thrust were all that could be desired.

On the other hand the change in propulsion system affected handling, and this is something immediately noticed by every pilot. A completely clean FGR2 comes near to having a cg (centre of gravity) problem. In a modern fighter designed to CCV (control-configured vehicle) concepts an aft cg is part of the design objective, but in a traditional fighter it puts a great strain on the jock in the front seat. At high weights it is difficult to avoid pio's (pilot-induced oscillations), in which the pilot is forever trying to damp out the switchback motion in pitch (technically called a phugoid) and only succeeding in making it worse. The problem is particularly acute on a maximum-endurance sortie involving inflight refuelling to near maximum weight, when with the probe in the basket the vertical motion is only too evident and without great concentration can lead to repeated unplanned disconnects. Pitch stability is improved by carrying live or dummy Sparrows in the front pair of recesses, so these are seldom seen empty.

In practice the left front (No 1) Sparrow recess is quite often largely empty, for the good reason that its rearmost section is the location for the removable strike camera. This is a plain ciné camera which can be switched on when required to record each run on a surface target, looking obliquely downwards. It can also be aimed to look ahead in the air-to-air mode. No aiming reticle appears on the film, but a replay does show where rockets or shells from a gun pod are actually hitting, besides giving a fair idea of where dropped stores would have landed.

By modern standards the FGR2 nav/attack kit looks distinctly dated, but with a good radar and INS the all-weather capability was excellent for its time. One obvious missing item is a HUD, and this has consistently been a question of money. As far as possible the RAF Phantoms have been modified to cope without one, and with an overall equipment fit which in the 1960s was quite comprehensive the result is still a capable and well-liked weapon platform. Of course, at all times the weapon capability has been extremely good by any standard. The five main pylons are stressed for an aggregate load exceeding 16,000lb whilst still preserving the structural manoeuvre limit of 7.75g, though this is seldom used in practice. A normal maximum is 11 free-fall or retarded bombs of 1,000lb nominal size, which in practice means a true weight nearer to 12,000lb. A normal total of 126 SNEB rockets of 68mm armour-piercing type is an alternative, and for many missions the SUU-23 gun pod is carried on the centreline.

Though this pod has some capability in the air-to-air role, it is used chiefly for hitting both soft and hard surface targets, and an adjective commonly applied to it is 'fab'. Containing the same Vulcan type 20mm gun as used on many US fighters, it actually has the self-powered GAU-4 model of this gun, with an electric inertia starter for initial spin-up to give the full firing rate of 6,000rpm almost the moment the trigger is depressed. The drum behind the gun contains 1,200 rounds, with a linkless feed. Use of the self-powered gun means firing rate does not fall away at low airspeeds, as it does with other versions. Though accuracy is bound to be inferior to that from an internal gun, the pod mounting is highly regarded and most pilots could put about 80% of the rounds fired into a single truck target. Live firing is possible on several ranges, including Larkhill and against rafts at Episcopi Bay during annual APC (Armament Practice Camp). Each squadron spends

Right:
The first combat squadron to equip with the FGR2 was No 6, whose can-opener badge resulted from their good trade in the Western Desert with the Hurricane IID with 40mm guns. Coningsby was obviously enjoying a rare spell of hot weather. In the rear Victor K1As of No 57 Squadron which tanked up the new fighters en route. *MoD(RAF)*

a month at RAF Akrotiri honing its weapon skills to qualify for the ACE (Allied Command Europe) proficiency standard.

Attack missions are discussed further in the chapter on strike/attack units in RAF Germany. It was expected that reconnaissance would become the chief secondary mission for the FGR2, and EMI was contracted to produce the appropriate pod (in the USAF and Marines this task is assigned to purpose-built Phantoms with no combat capability). Using a lot of technology from the cancelled TSR2 programme EMI created the biggest, most capable and most expensive recon pod of the 1960s. To reduce carriage problems the external size and shape were made roughly the same as that of the 500gal (2,271litre, 600 US gal) tank which is an alternative

store on the centreline. Equipment included forward, vertical and oblique cameras, I/J-band SLAR (sideways-looking aircraft radar) and IR linescan. Pods were made by BAe (then Hawker Siddeley) at Brough, and they were carried by 41 Sqn in the UK and 2 (II) Sqn in RAFG. For various reasons the pods were withdrawn and most have been dismantled, and some of the contents were built into the smaller recon pods carried by the Jaguars with which II Sqn is now equipped. In contrast, back in 1972 the Phantom was regarded as vital as an all-weather recon platform, and it was announced that the change in defence policy, which was to result in Phantoms switching en mass to the air-defence role, applied to every FGR2 except those engaged in the recon mission!

When the Phantom entered RAF service it initially replaced the Hunter in No 38 Group, Air Support Command. Crews trained by 228 OCU were posted to form the nucleus of No 6 Sqn, also at Conningsby,

Above:
Initial deliveries of the FGR2 went to No 228 OCU, which was re-formed in October 1968 at Coningsby to train crews for the Phantom squadrons. The second aircraft along is XT891, the first production RAF Phantom, that in the foreground being the third. Note the use of two ladders per aircraft — and the keep of Tattershall Castle in the background. *Martin Horseman*

which re-formed on 7 May 1969 as the first FGR2 squadron. It operated Phantoms until 1 October 1974, by which time it had completed conversion to the Jaguar GR1 at Lossiemouth (subsequently at Coltishall). No 54 Sqn formed in 38 Group at West Raynham on 1 September 1969, and likewise flew the FGR2 until 23 April 1974 by which time it had become a Jaguar unit. The third 38 Group Phantom strike/recon squadron was No 41, which re-formed (taking its famous number from a Bloodhound SAM unit) on 1 April 1972. No 41 was based most of its Phantom life at Coningsby, and specialised in reconnaissance using the EMI pod.

Above:
XV432 burdened by the following stores: two 360gal tanks; three Sparrow AIM-7E radar-guided AAMs; six SNEB rocket pods; the strike camera in the forward left missile recess; and the centreline gun pod. *MoD(RAF)*

Below:
For comparison, here is a different weapon loading, demonstrated by XV407 of No 41 Sqn, also based at Coningsby: two 360gal tanks; four AIM-7E Sparrow missiles; four BL755 cluster bomb dispensers; and the multisensor reconnaissance pod. *MoD(RAF)*

O

437

Above left:
No 54 Sqn operated the FGR2 as an element of 38 Group, Air Support Command, based at West Raynham. Aircraft 'O' was XV475, seen here clean except for pylons. The four auxiliary engine-bay doors are all open. *Martin Horseman*

Left:
This portrait of XV437 shows that No 54 Sqn also on occasion carried the reconnaissance pod, other stores here including two tanks, two Sparrows, two dark blue dummy Sparrows carried in the front recesses to bring the cg forward, and four SNEB pods. *MoD(RAF)*

Above:
Taken over a cloud layer above St Omer, northern France, this October 1975 picture clearly shows the strike camera (under the roundel). Pilot and navigator of this 41 Sqn aircraft are more interested in the photo aircraft. *MoD(RAF)*

Below:
It is SOP (standard operating procedure) to stream the braking parachute on landing. The wheel brakes are generally regarded as prone to hydraulic failure, and it is not uncommon for electric failure to remove nosewheel steering, and this 228 OCU instructor (in XV409) may well be saying 'Always regard the hook as a bonus.' *Martin Horseman*

XLI
RESCUE
XLI
RESCUE

Left:
In contrast to two ladders per aircraft, No 41 Sqn had only one ladder in place on this row of four, and any F-4 jock will tell you that both crew-members can get aboard using the aircraft's own retractable steps, clearly seen here. The nearest aircraft is XV490, and the furthest 401. *Martin Horseman*

Top:
Scramble by a pair of FGR2s from 228 OCU, whose alternative designation is 64 Sqn, a famous fighter unit whose scarab emblem appears in the centre of 228's tail insignia. The aircraft are XV474 and XV398. *Martin Horseman*

Above:
Real hustle on the apron at Coningsby as XV492 of 6 Sqn is refuelled, rearmed, serviced and got rolling again in eight minutes. The vehicle registered 29AG02 is the Sparrow missile loader. After the aircraft is parked, the inflight-refuelling probe is kept out for a visual inspection. *MoD(RAF)*

Left:
At the far western end of Coningsby airfield is this well-equipped 'hush house' where even a Spey in full reheat causes no environmental noise problem. Well strapped down, with mesh guards over the inlets, is 228 OCU's XV472, pictured on another page. *Martin Horseman*

Below left:
XV482 of 6 Sqn undergoes landing-gear cycling tests during normal hangar maintenance. Hydraulic and electric power is supplied from the ground. *Martin Horseman*

Below:
XV483 of 41 Sqn pictured on a low-level sortie over France, with wing tanks, two practice bomb carriers (four 28lb bombs), centreline gun pod, one ballast missile and the strike camera. *MoD(RAF)*

Right:
XV492 'Q' of 6 Sqn parked at Coningsby with wing tanks, gun pod and strike camera. Tidy parking is ensured by twin painted lines for the nosewheels to follow. *Martin Horseman*

Below right:
XV488 from 228 OCU, with fin-cap ECM added, makes a slow fly-past with hook down at the Open Day at RAF Abingdon in September 1979. It is carrying ballast Sparrows and dummy Sidewinders. *MoD(RAF)*

RESCUE
492

4

RAF STRIKE COMMAND: AIR DEFENCE

Right:
The first Phantom air-defence unit in the RAF was No 43 Sqn, the 'Fighting Cocks', who re-formed on 1 September 1969 to fly the FG.1 originally intended for the Royal Navy. Based at Leuchars, four were photographed in 1970 passing the Forth bridges. *MoD(RAF)*

In 1972 a major RAF reorganisation took place, completed on 1 September of that year. It affected mainly Strike Command, which today embraces virtually all the tactical airpower of the service outside Germany. Greatly increased emphasis was put on air defence, and whereas in 1957 this was confidently expected to be handled solely by SAMs, plans were made to transfer to this role all the Phantoms in the UK and for the longer term to procure a special air-defence version (ADV) of the Tornado. To a considerable degree this was made possible by the entry into service from June 1973 of the Jaguar, which in the UK replaced the Phantom in 6, 41 and 54 Sqns and released these aircraft for the air-defence role.

There is no room in this book for politics, but the change in organisation and emphasis stemmed from the abandonment of the nuclear 'tripwire' policy, under which the number of interceptor aircraft based in the UK was allowed to fall to a mere 60 — the lowest since 1916 — in favour of so-called 'flexible response', with substantial improvements in conventional forces. The UK ADR (Air Defence Region), part of NATO Early Warning Area 12, is a large volume of sky stretching as far west as Iceland and eastwards to the Baltic, and intrusions by probing aircraft of the Soviet air forces have become virtually a daily occurrence. The short-legged Lightning was never designed for operations within such a large region, and in 1974 the Lightning OCU was closed (though the LTF, Lightning Training Flight, was still active in mid-1983).

In its place the former 228 OCU became tasked with air-defence training, while at the same busy airfield of Coningsby were built up two FGR2 air-defence squadrons, Nos 29 and 111, the latter moving to Leuchars on 3 November 1975. Long before this, on 1 September 1969, No 43 Sqn, the 'Fighting Cocks', had been re-formed on the surplus FG1s not assigned to the Royal Navy. Based at Leuchars, it was tasked from the start with air defence, especially of naval forces, and is probably the only Phantom unit to have remained since that time at the same base and with the same task. In its early years it operated alongside the Navy's POCU. It was joined at Leuchars by 23 Sqn, which relinquished its Lightnings and disbanded on 30 October 1975, to re-form 18 days later on the FGR2. No 23 moved on 25 February 1976 to Wattisham. Here it joined the last member of the Phantom home-defence team, No 56, which had brought its Lightnings back from Cyprus in January 1975 prior to re-equipment.

In the early 1970s the disappointing performance of the Spey-Phantom at medium and high altitudes was regarded as serious, but over the years the high-flying threat is judged to have receded, and today a far more dangerous presence is the 600-odd Su-24 'Fencer' long-range interdiction aircraft which would certainly operate at the lowest possible level. Here the Phantom is as good as the Lightning in general performance, though for a time the RAF carefully studied ways of reducing weight — even to the extent of tearing out the inertial navigation system — in order to pull more g and reduce the turn radius. Of course, compared with the Lightning there is absolutely no contest when it comes to radar and weapons, and with the excellent pulse-doppler AWG-11/12 radar and eight AAMs, four of them of the medium-range radar-guided type, the FGR.2 is an extremely useful all-weather interceptor with plenty of what is today called 'combat persistence'. This means it can keep on firing at different targets, or even at the same target if it is unlucky enough not to score with the first shot. Certainly the concept of four big AAMs recessed under the fuselage plus four close-range weapons on external pylons set a completely new level of armament when the Phantom introduced it in 1958. Suffice to say it is good enough for Strike Command's air-defence Phantom squadrons often to fly without the gun pod (which is an important air-defence weapon), and we do not hear too much clamour about lack of an internal gun.

Of course, the Tornado F2 beats the tough old St Louis product in all departments, not only in weapons (plus internal gun) but most notably in avionics and displays and also in low fuel consumption. But this book is not intended to eulogise the Phantom's successor!

In the interception role there is not a lot of difference between the FGR2 and 43 Sqn's FG1, though the latter has a slightly different radar and lacks the inertial system and HF radio. As it is a feature of all FGR2s the HF set could be discussed in any of several chapters, but it cannot be ignored because chaps coming to the Phantom FGR2 from other aircraft are usually amazed to be able to get clear voice reception half-way around the world. Crews have talked to Support Command at Upavon whilst at wavetop height in full afterburner north of the Shetlands or parked on the apron at Akrotiri (Cyprus), whilst during the deployments to Singapore-Tengah (now sadly discontinued, to save money) it was common to talk to Tengah from the Aden/Gan area.

All the home air-defence Phantom squadrons are part of the famous No 11 Group, whose HQ is still at Bentley Priory despite the tragic burning down of

Above right:
Over the flat Lincolnshire fields the then-new FGR2s of No 111 Sqn practice formation flying on first converting from Lightnings in July 1974. Fuel can stream from the wing vents, and from the dual tail vent (which, as noted earlier, is shorter on Spey Phantoms) whenever tanks or system pressure rises significantly above ambient. This often happens on takeoff. Two of the aircraft are also making tip vortex trails, but these are faint. *MoD(RAF)*

the original Priory in 1980. All units spend one month each year at Armament Practice Camp at Akrotiri, usually with a non-stop transit with an inflight-refuelling en route. Here there is fine weather and a clear sea area where many kinds of mission can be flown, including visual interception and live firing with the gun pod against Canberra-towed banners. AAMs are not fired, for the simple reason that there is no money to buy replacements, but simulated AAM attacks are possible in the UK because they are purely electronic.

There are various 'weapon' loads in the air-to-air training role. Plain dark-blue Sparrows are ballast, to reduce the problem of instability in pitch referred to earlier. These serve no training function, but merely pull the cg forward and reduce the drag of the empty AAM recesses. For training it is usual to insert a 'sim plug' (simulation plug) which provides exactly the same system inputs as a real Sparrow or Sky Flash. In the same way it is common to fly with Sidewinder training missiles which often look like a mere piece of pipe. Some STMs have the rolleron-equipped fins of the real missile, though they are not released and have an inert motor and simulated warhead. What they do have is a real IR homing head, which can be switched on, refrigerated, cued by the radar towards a target, locked-on and taken through the complete interception so that the pilot can become familiar with the way the seeker head's growling in his headphones rises to a high-pitched singing as it closes on a target, or as the target's apparent thermal emissions increase. Thus the problem of firing too soon, or failing to fire at the earliest certain moment, can be avoided by repeated practice without consuming costly missiles.

Today the Phantoms are painted grey and have ECM fin-top installations which alter the appearance. These developments are discussed later.

Below:
Arrival of an FG1 of 43 Sqn at RAF Luqa, Malta, with the familiar cathedral in the background. Today RAF combat aircraft are rarely able to visit the sunny island. *MoD(RAF)*

Top:
Return to Coningsby of an FGR2, XV403, of 'Treble-One' squadron. In the early 1970s underwing roundels were three-colour.

Above:
Four Sidewinders and a partly-assembled Sparrow ready to go aboard XV442 of No 29 Sqn at Coningsby in January 1975. Those familiar with the 'other kind of F-4' around the world will notice the enlarged inlet ducts. *MoD(RAF)*

Above:
With tailplanes at full negative incidence an FG1 of the 'Fighting Cocks' (43) lands at Greenham Common during an International Air Tattoo in the mid-1970s. The upper rod projecting ahead of the fin is the ASI pitot head; the lower is a ram inlet to serve the flight-control q-feel system, which reduces the surface movement for a given pilot input as the aircraft descends into denser air, thus preventing coarse demands from breaking the aircraft. *Martin Horseman*

Below:
XV490, Sidewinders aboard, is given the 'halt' command after a practice sortie from Coningsby in NBC (nuclear/biological/chemical) conditions. The unit is 29 Sqn. *Martin Horseman*

Top:
After a few hours an NBC exercise is heartily disliked — but perhaps nothing like as much as the real thing. Perspiring and probably tired, the crew of XV490 pass down their impedimenta before leaving the aircraft. *Martin Horseman*

Above:
Having converted from Lightnings to Phantoms, No 23 Sqn moved in early 1976 to Wattisham, Suffolk. Here a technician checks the ballast Sparrows on XT912 during the changeover from Lightnings at Leuchars. *Martin Horseman*

Top:
The Falklands again demonstrated the importance to the RAF of flight refuelling. Here Phantoms of No 29 Sqn, which nine years later flew to the Falklands using the technique, practice with Victor K1A XA936 of 214 Sqn, now disbanded. *IAL*

Above:
A full load of Sparrows and STMs (Sidewinder training missiles) on another aircraft of 111 Sqn, apparently XV418, on a training sortie on 8 August 1974. *MoD(RAF)*

Above:
We make no apology for including this, one of a series of similar well-known posed groups taken in July 1974, because they show the whole kit of air defence weapons: Sidewinders, Sparrows and SUU-23 gun pod and ammunition. XV478 was with 111 Sqn, then still at Coningsby *MoD(RAF)*

Above right:
XV401 of No 56 Squadron, Wattisham, taxies out on a training mission under a cloudless sky. This was one of the first aircraft to receive one of the few visible mods, an extra mirror for the navigator giving a view straight back along the top of the fuselage, visible in most illustrations from here on. *Robert F. Dorr*

Right:
Phantoms of 56 Sqn parked at RAF Leuchars during a tactical fighter meet in May 1978. XV482 bears the R badge of Luftwaffe JG71 *Richthofen* wing because it is flown by one of the squadron's regular German exchange crews, usually from JG71 *MoD(RAF)*

401
N

C

D
D
432

Above left:
Leuchars is one of the UK stations to have blast walls to give some protection to parked aircraft, in this case XT874, an FG1 of 43 Sqn. Note use of aircraft letter on nose-gear door instead of serial number. *Martin Horseman*

Left:
No 23 Sqn are helpful enough to paint both the serial and aircraft letter on the nose gear. The 16ft ring-slot chute is the same as on other people's Phantoms. *Martin Horseman*

Above and right:
Two photographs taken at Coningsby on 21 July 1979 prior to a training mission by a crew of 29 Sqn aboard aircraft 'F' (XV422). The close-up shows the rear-view mirrors inside the canopy, the projecting AOA probe and the left-hand ram-air inlet for avionics cooling. *Michael France*

ROYAL AIR FORCE
1919-ROLLS-ROYCE EAGLE
1979-ROLLS-ROYCE SPEY
TRANSATLANTIC FLIGHT

Above left:
This says it all — almost! No 23 repainted XV434, with Rolls-Royce sponsorship, for a 5hr 40min flight from Labrador to Greenham Common to celebrate the 60th anniversary of the first non-stop aeroplane flight across the Atlantic by Alcock and Brown in 1919. The date was 21 June 1979, and pilot Sqn Ldr A. J. H. (Tony) Alcock MBE was the nephew of the 1919 Sir John. Backseater Flt Lt Norman Browne did a good job despite the e on his name. *23 Sqn*

Left:
Live missiles are carried on missions which intercept and identify 'Zombies' (Soviet aircraft approaching the UK). In this case an FGR2 of 111 Sqn, still lacking external mirror, shepherds a 'Bear-D' in early 1980. *MoD(RAF)*

Top:
ECM fin caps began to appear in 1979. Here fully armed XV469, aircraft A of 56 Sqn, taxies out at Wattisham on 16 April 1980. *MoD(RAF)*

Above:
The Leuchars apron in May 1980 occupied by FGR2s of 111 and FG1s of 43. Note trollied Sidewinders. At the far end are visiting Luftwaffe RF-4Es. *MoD(RAF)*

Above:
A fully updated aircraft of 56 Sqn flying with four STMs and four Sparrows painted with locally applied B-type roundels. Photograph 1980 (no precise date). *MoD(RAF)*

Below:
Close-up of Treble-One insignia, Mk 7 seat, right-side ram inlet (cockpit refrigeration) and nose of ballast Sparrow. *MoD(RAF)*

Right:
Sidewinders are loaded manually. Here AIM-9B (Update) missiles go aboard an aircraft of 23 Sqn during Exercise 'Elder Forest 80', with everyone in NBC garb. *Martin Horseman*

Below right:
The Sparrow loader can handle the 452lb missiles, but NBC rubber gloves make precise alignment hard to achieve. Note the exit grille for cooling air bled from the engines and blown between the titanium inner skin and aluminium outer skin. More cooling air enters at the base of the fin. *MoD(RAF)*

WARNING

Above:
NBC 'decontamination' at Wattisham during 'Elder Forest 80'. Similar operations are mounted to wash away fuel spillage, which commonly occurs from the trailing-edge pipes if a tanked-up Phantom is left in hot sunshine. *Martin Horseman*

Above right:
The FG1s delivered new to the RAF did not have the tailplane incidence scale. Aircraft 'D' of No 43 Sqn (XV576) also lacked the external navigator mirror when this was taken in 1981. *Martin Horseman*

Right:
XT903 flew up to BAe Warton from 64 Sqn (228 OCU) on the occasion of the roll-out of the first Tornado F2. Since then the Phantom's partner and eventual successor in the air-defence role has been cleared for service, and is in production. *Martin Horseman*

D

TORNADO
F-2

895

Left:
The top of a Coningsby apron floodlight tower is lost in the murk on a wet day in January 1975. The aircraft had just been assigned to the re-formed No 29 Sqn. *MoD(RAF)*

Below left:
Reheat departure of XV579, one of the FG1s of No 43 Sqn, with the auxiliary air doors closed; date May 1980. *MoD(RAF)*

Right:
Tail detail of an FGR2 of No 111 Sqn, in July 1974. Note the arrester hook, fuel system vent (above the drag chute door) and the tailplane pivot, well above the surface itself. *MoD(RAF)*

Below:
Scramble by a 23 Sqn aircraft from Wattisham in March 1982. *MoD(RAF)*

5

RAF GERMANY: ATTACK/ RECONNAISSANCE

Below:
In 1972-3 the Spey was having terrible problems, and squadrons suffered the humility of being grounded, but here 20 tons of thrust comes on each of the 31 Sqn aircraft with no problem. *Martin Horseman*

RAF Germany, part of the 2nd ATAF (Allied Tactical Air Force), is totally committed to NATO's Central Front, and is thus considered to be 'at the sharp end' of Western defence. The first Phantom FGR2s to join RAFG replaced Canberra B(I)8s of 14 (previously numbered 88) Sqn at Brüggen, on 30 June 1970. From that day the FGR2 enjoyed a fairly brief spell of five years in the strike/attack role, with one outfit — 'shiny II' — also dedicated to reconnaissance. By 1976 all the Phantom attack squadrons had converted to the Jaguar, though some Phantoms continued flying with RAFG squadrons well into 1977.

No 2 (II) AC (Army Co-operation) Squadron proudly traces its history back to the earliest days of the Royal Flying Corps, for it was formed on 13 May 1912. It was almost 60 years later that it converted from the Hunter FR10 to the Phantom, and very remarkably it did not receive the EMI reconnaissance pod until May 1976, by which time several of its aircraft had the fin-cap ECM installation. Throughout, the unit has been based at RAF Laarbruch, sharing the station with Nos 15 and 16 Squadron Buccaneers. The costly reconnaissance pod hardly gave value for money with No 2, because it was in use for barely a year. It is questionable that the switch to the Jaguar has meant any significant diminution in reconnaissance capability, because the much smaller Jaguar pod carries five oblique cameras and IR linescan and has closely similar coverage. Indeed the greater weight of the pod carried by the Phantom ate more severely into the possible payloads of other stores, though it was always possible with the FGR2 to carry 'a full suite' of either air defence or ground attack weapons, or a mixture. Conversely, the last photograph taken of an FGR2 with 'shiny II' shows it with the gun pod instead of the recon pod.

The other RAFG attack squadrons were Nos 14, 17 and 31, which together made up the Brüggen wing. In each case the American fighter replaced the Canberra, the attack B(I)8 in the case of No 14, the unarmed PR3 in the case of No 17 and the slightly more powerful and longer-ranged PR7 with No 31. This meant a change of role for the last two units, the PR Canberras having had no weapon capability. No 17 was re-formed on Phantoms on 16 September 1970, but No 31 did not convert from Canberras until well into 1972, so it had only quite a short innings before receiving its first Jaguar three years later. All units in the Brüggen wing converted to the Jaguar in the course of 1975-6, No 31 finally being declared operational on the European aircraft in July 1976.

Any air combat unit on the NATO Central Sector has to be able to hack it in close combat, possibly against vastly superior numbers of aircraft. In the case of the Phantom there was clearly the probability of facing opponents who were much more agile, because the British Phantom has always retained the original wing with blown droops instead of the powerful manoeuvring slats of the F-4E. Germany is psychologically a demanding area, with all kinds of weather, lots of air traffic, and the presence of colossal Warsaw Pact forces within a few minutes flying time.

These reasons help to explain an emphasis on night and bad weather mission training, though of course the Phantom lacks a TFR and, with only a radar altimeter to ensure safe separation from the ground, the cockpit workload is high. This is as good a place as any to emphasise the absolute reliance of the pilot on the GIB (guy in the back), who in the RAF is officially called the navigator. His most vital function during the crucial phases of a night or bad-weather attack is to use at least two of the seven or eight eyes in his head to look outside the cockpit, monitor the pitch attitude and keep at least one eye on the radar altimeter, and yell 'Pull up!' should this ever be absolutely essential. It is not at all uncommon for the pilot to become dangerously disorientated, and it may not be too much to claim that half the RAF Phantoms might have 'gone straight in' had there been no GIB. Certainly there is no Phantom pilot who would dispute the assertion that the navigators earn their pay.

Another of the tasks of the GIB is to manage the radar. Though the radar displays are duplicated, almost all the radar controls are in the rear cockpit, and it would be virtually impossible for a pilot to fly an effective mission by himself. A skilled pilot can, for example, control an air interception alone and can do various instructive demonstrations for a pupil navigator, but on a real combat mission a pilot with no navigator might as well stay on the ground. Another area almost solely in the hands of the backseater is EW (electronic warfare). The ARI18228 passive RWR (radar warning receiver), whose aerials are inside the fin-cap fairing added since the mid-1970s, presents its information in the form of bright radial lines on a small CRT (cathode-ray tube) in the rear cockpit. Like many RWRs, it gives a useful broad-brush directional indication of each enemy emitter, though it is by no means a new installation and has little to say about the enemy emissions themselves, or their probable identity.

EW is clearly a sensitive area, but it is equally clearly one in which the RAF has declined from being No 1 in the world in the mid-1940s to being very much an also-ran in the 1980s. No aircraft has greater need of a modern computer-controlled high-power EW system than a ground-attack Phantom on the Central Sector, but the author has no information on anything being done at all. A few years ago the RAF managed to find a little money to buy second-hand ALQ-101 jammer pods from the USAF in Europe, but these appear to have been issued only to Buccaneer squadrons. Whether money will be found for any comprehensive suite of jammers and payload dispensers for the Phantoms is anybody's guess. Bearing in mind the disgraceful way chaff bundles had to be jammed between bombs and ejector racks on Falklands Harriers one hopes the Phantoms can do better. Their crews deserve it.

Training in ground attack missions in Germany is far from easy. There is hardly anywhere that bombs can actually be dropped, and Phantoms often visit the ranges at Wainfleet (off Lincolnshire) or Sardinia. Even use of Lepus flares at night is very restricted, because in dry weather a low-level flare can start a brush fire. In a typical night attack mission six aircraft might be detailed, a nominated Flare Ship having six Lepus on two triple stations. This will lead the others in loose trail at low level, using Tacan and AI radar (pulse or pulse doppler), keeping closer station as the target is approached. At the last moment the lead navigator will switch to GM (ground map) radar mode to paint the target, the pilot making any necessary steering corrections from his own head-down cockpit display. Radar predicted maps are used wherever the terrain is familiar and such maps exist. The lead navigator will order a pull-up at 4g for a toss manoeuvre, calling 'pickle' at the exact moment for flare release, at a predetermined climb angle of about 25°. On a major target all six Lepus may be released at once. Then the drill is to roll 140° from the top of the zoom and pull back close to ground level and away. The other five aircraft will attack with bombs, SNEBs, or even gunfire.

Phantom crews quickly attain the kind of cool proficiency for which the RAF has always been justly famous. They can do a good job with the Phantom, and are naturally attached to their tough and versatile bird. But so do other crews love their portly 'Buccs', and it has to be admitted that both aircraft, which represented the major part of the RAF's tactical airpower until 1984, are as outdated as the ark in comparison with a modern type such as the Tornado. It is partly for this reason that Phantoms have been switched from attack to defence, because in the latter role there are fewer avionic shortages.

Below:
The CO of 31 Sqn and two wingmen move out for a training exercise at Brüggen. XV501 (right rear) was the last RAF aircraft, delivered on 29 August 1969. *Martin Horseman*

Top:
An FGR2 of 31 Sqn goes through Brüggen's nuclear-decontamination facility in April 1974. Ordinary mains water is used, though on occasion soap and brooms are brought out. *MoD(RAF)*

Above:
A quartet from 31 Sqn practice low level over the countryside near the Dutch border. All RAFG Phantoms in the strike/recon role had the serial number in white on the fin. *MoD(RAF)*

Above right:
An aircraft of 17 Sqn banks away during the NATO Tactical Weapons Meet held at Baden Soellingen in June 1974. The RAF Phantom team turned in the highest score among the seven NATO air forces competing, and assisted 2ATAF to win. Note centreline gun, practice-bomb carriers, ballast Sparrow and strike camera. *MoD(RAF)*

Right:
A Phantom from 17 Sqn participated in the 'opening ceremony' of the first hardened aircraft shelter at RAF Brüggen, on 16 October 1974. *MoD(RAF)*

498

489

Above:
Another aircraft from 17 Sqn was called upon to taxi across the 'filled-in bomb crater' to show the proficiency of 52 Field Sqn (Airfields), Royal Engineers, before the SACEUR Evaluation Team at RAF Wildenrath in November 1974. *BAOR*

Below:
One aircraft from each of the squadrons in the Brüggen wing: XV419 (14 Sqn) flanked by XV497 (17 Sqn) and XV433 (31 Sqn), in April 1975. *RAFG*

Above:
August 1975 photograph showing the two types then equipping 14 Sqn — and the two COs, Wg Cdr Derek Hine flying the Phantom and the incoming CO, Wg Cdr Anthony Mumford, the Jaguar. *RAFG*

Below:
XV498 of 17 Sqn demonstrates the 100th arrested landing made at RAF Brüggen, using the All American Engineering cable-drum system originally developed for the US Marine Corps. *RAFG via IAL*

Above:
Carrying a gun pod instead of a recon pod, XV468, ex-II AC Sqn, joins Wildenrath in February 1977 to fly on air defence with 19 Sqn. *RAFG*

DO NOT REMOVE WITH POD CRUTCHED

898

Above left:
No 2 (No II AC) Squadron painted shark's teeth and eyes on their first reconnaissance pod in June 1976. Note strike camera and, in the background, the next-generation Jaguar. *RAFG*

Left:
XT898 of 'Shiny II' got its ECM fin cap before it got a recon pod! Note also the HASs in the background, by June 1976 a familiar part of the Laarbruch landscape. *RAFG*

Top:
First takeoff by a recon-pod Phantom in RAF Germany. *RAFG*

Above:
XV430 of No II AC takes its pod along the route of a future Autobahn. *Flight International*

6

RAF GERMANY: AIR DEFENCE

Below:
XN789, one of 19 Squadron's much-modified Lightning F2As, formating with the replacement aircraft (in this case XV484) on 14 December 1976. The Phantom is demonstrating a full kit of live missiles and the gun pod. *RAFG*

The fact that in RAF Germany the Phantom began as a ground attack aircraft, with one squadron also tasked with multisensor reconnaissance, whereas today the RAFG Phantoms are interceptors, merely serves to underscore the inherent versatility of this great aircraft. To switch from one role to another demands not only comprehensive avionics and equipment, and an exceptional spread of possible weapon fits, but also good all-round flight performance with no significant shortcoming.

In RAFG the two squadrons today are Nos 19 and 92, both at Wildenrath. Both previously were the sole operators of the unique Lightning F2A, which was basically a Lightning F2 rebuilt close to F6 standard. Originally unpainted, the Lightnings were later given an unusual colour scheme in which the upper surface was dark olive green all over, to reduce visibility on the ground to hostile aircraft. The Phantom FGR2s, however, were handed over after service with other RAFG squadrons in the attack/recon role, and at first retained standard grey/green camouflage. Both began to re-equip with the Phantom in 1976, No 19 getting the first aircraft on 27 September and No 92 a few days later.

While on the subject of colour schemes, RAF Central Trials & Tactics Division, at Strike Command HQ at High Wycombe, managed a prolonged investigation into suitable camouflage (or, in some cases, conspicuous markings) since the mid-1970s. To some extent notes were compared with the USAF and other NATO air forces, though true to NATO tradition there was never any agreement on finding a 'best scheme' to which the 15 nations could adhere. So each country has not only its own numerical code designations for identical shades but also a completely different set of colour schemes from most of the others. In some cases attempts to touch up visiting aircraft have resulted in what, at best, could be called a near miss. But since 1979 all Phantoms operating in the air-defence role, which means practically every example in the RAF, has been due to be repainted — as major overhauls or other opportunities arise — in standard matt Light Aircraft Grey. This greatly reduces air-to-air visibility in many European conditions, but is proving difficult to keep clean.

In the air-combat role the radar is the absolutely dominant item of kit, without which a mission might as well be aborted, As emphasised previously, the AWG-11/12 was a very sophisticated radar for its day (and that day is long gone because, though updated since, Westinghouse in Baltimore had virtually completed its design in 1960). In particular, its pulse-doppler mode is so good against low-flying bogeys that the RAF Phantom is significantly better than, for example, F-4Es of the USAF or F-4Fs of the Luftwaffe in this role. On the other hand, the 11/12 is big, heavy and by modern standards unreliable, with an MTBF generally less than half as long as for the small aircooled radar of the F-16. On the other hand the whole bulky package pulls out on rails, so that replacing any of the LRUs (line-replaceable units, commonly called black boxes) presents no problem.

At present the only other interceptors on the Central Sector with a high-power pulse-doppler radar are the USAF F-15s of the 36th TFW at Bitburg and 32nd TFS at Camp New Amsterdam. As MAC's next-generation fighter after the F-4 this could hardly fail to be superior, but the old FGR2s of the 19th and 92nd squadrons are regarded as worthy partners. In the tough German sky the action is essentially all at low level, and the situation could hardly fail to be a multi-bogey one. This is in contrast to the Phantom squadrons back home in the UK, where, except in the south-east approaches, Warsaw Pact fighters are not expected to be seen.

Thus for 19 and 92 air combat is a very essential part of their training, and they try to get good enough to give a fair account of themselves when up against such specialists as the USAF 327th Aggressor Sqn. A particularly important NATO facility is the ACMI (air-combat manoeuvring instrumentation) range at Decimomannu, Sardinia, where ground recorders faithfully tape each pilot's visual sight and the complete air-combat parameters of flight speed, AOA (angle of attack) and height, and can play back a complete air combat in the form of TV tableaux. Each pilot can see for himself what gun or AAM success or failure he would have had in a real combat. In the past, to some extent, the fighter jock who could argue the loudest, or the most convincingly, used to win. Not no more! Deci cuts out the arguments and brutally lays bare the deficiencies.

For reasons of fuel burn it is obviously undesirable to fly complete missions at low level, and it is common to fly CAP from about 15 to 25k (15,000 to 25,000ft altitude). This is a flight level at which the FGR2 still has fair performance, and it can stooge about burning slightly less fuel than an F-4E, and can certainly acquire all sorts of targets from greater distances. Thus the BVR (beyond visual range) AAM is a very important part of the weapon fit, and another big plus on the side of the RAF is the replacement of Sparrows by the Sky Flash, which is a British weapon developed by BAe Dynamics by mating a Sparrow airframe with a far superior MSDS microelectronic homing head.

Sky Flash, then called XJ521, was put through its initial test firing programme at US Navy Air Station Pt Mugu, with firings over the Pacific Missile Test Range and the overland China Lake range, using two hired F-4Js. With abundant safety parameters on the huge ranges, superb instrumentation and good weather, the programme went like a dream; it was easily the most successful ever flown at Pt Mugu. Every missile either struck its target or passed within lethal distance despite the greatest efforts of the

Above:
The same Phantom, 484, is seen again in fully armed condition, but this time in January 1977. *RAFG*

testers to confuse it by injecting heavy jamming and other kinds of ECM. Targets included a QF-86, QT-33s, a QF-4B and a former Bomarc SAM cruising at Mach 4 at far above the height any fighter could fly. Multi-target trials were flown, including a discrimination test in which two QT-33s flew in the tightest possible formation.

Though AIM-7E is still in use, Sky Flash is today widely deployed with the Phantom squadrons, and is considered a really major advance. At the same time, it is still an SARH (semi-active radar homing) weapon, requiring its target to be illuminated by the Phantom throughout the missile's flight. This can be a great drawback, because it rapidly closes the range in a way that would otherwise be considered unnecessary and suicidal. For years it has been recognised that the 'fire and forget' BVR missile is what is needed, and while BAe Dynamics and other European partners (and the USA's Hughes) work on Asraam, the next-generation short-range weapon, the USA is far advanced with Amraam, Advanced medium-range AAM, called AIM-120A in the US services. This will begin to replace Sparrow and eventually Sky Flash from about 1985.

The stalwart FGR2s will remain in service long after that time, even though by that year the superb Tornado F2 will reach the RAF squadrons. Compared with the Phantom, the F2 will offer similar weapon capability plus an internal gun, higher all-round flight performance, dramatically reduced fuel burn and thus greater CAP endurance, and an avionics standard that is out of this world, and really makes the toughest interception seem easy. Unfortunately for the FGR2 squadrons, the Tornados will get Amraam first.

498

Left:
A mix of squadron markings at Wildenrath in February 1977 as two Phantoms of 19 Sqn (XV468 still with II AC insignia) scramble on a practice interception. *RAFG*

Below left:
RAF Germany crews concentrate on low-level work, and normally carry the gun pod as valuable in close combat. Here aircraft 'J' of 19 Sqn returns to Wildenrath in February 1977. *RAFG*

Right:
Aircraft 'A' of 19 Sqn (XV497) returns from a mission. In the background can be seen giant rolls of aluminium matting used by the Royal Engineers to form instant runways or cover bomb craters. *RAFG via IAL*

Below:
Two Phantoms of No 92 Squadron seen in August 1979. That nearer the camera has the external mirror but no ECM fin-cap, and has yet to receive squadron insignia. *RAFG*

W

Above:
An aircraft of 92 Sqn photographed through the canopy of another during a low-level run over the North Sea in August 1979. *RAFG*

Top:
Though it is January 1980 these aircraft from the two RAFG air-defence squadrons have yet to be fitted with either the extra mirror or the ECM fin cap. *RAFG*

Above:
The official caption to this January 1980 picture omitted to refer to the Spitfire VB! Aircraft of both squadrons are visible, XV484 in the foreground being armed with live missiles. *RAFG*

Above:
Fitted with the new ILS aerial on the fin, this FGR2 was one of the first to appear in the low-visibility colour scheme. There are still reservations about this scheme, because it is less than ideal on the ground or at the low levels at which RAF Germany habitually operates. *RAFG*

Below:
This echelon of 92 Sqn aircraft includes one aircraft painted in the then-new standard finish of pale grey overall. Taken in January 1980 it shows aircraft at annual practice camp in Cyprus, flying over the Mediterranean. *RAFG*

Right:
In landing configuration, XV487, a Phantom of No 92 Sqn, turns over the River Humber before joining the glidepath to Holme on Spalding Moor for a major overhaul.
British Aerospace

Below:
Rotation point for a Phantom of 92 Sqn, and the slatted tailplanes go to full negative angle. The ailerons do not droop on the FGR2. *RAFG via IAL*

Below right:
On 18 June 1982, during Exercise TAM 82, these two aircraft of RAF No 92 Sqn were parked at Wittmundhafen beside one of the resident F-4Fs of JG 71. The 'Grey Goose' is XV460 and the traditional camouflaged machine XV471. *RAFG*

W
XV460

7

RAF PHANTOMS TODAY

Below:
XV589 is an FG1 now flying at Leuchars with 111 Sqn. It wears squadron markings, toned down in colours and much smaller than before, and in wartime these would be removed. Serial and other stencilling is in white, and in this case all roundels are small and three-colour. *RAF Leuchars*

Today the RAF has eight Phantom units: 29 Sqn at Coningsby, 43 at Leuchars, 56 at Wattisham, 111 at Leuchars and 228 OCU at Coningsby in the UK, 19 and 92 Sqns at Wildenrath in West Germany and 23 Sqn in the Falklands. These have an aggregate first-line strength of 87 aircraft, and all are tasked in the air-defence role. Virtually every Phantom is now painted grey overall, including the radome, and has the ECM fin cap.

Aesthetically, they probably look better and more purposeful than at any time in the past. B-type two-colour roundels are worn, with the corresponding two-colour fin flash. Colours are extremely subdued and are hardly distinguishable in some light conditions. There is still a remarkable degree of variation between the insignia of individual aircraft. Roundel and fin flash sizes are far from uniform, and 111 Sqn even has a penchant for the three-colour insignia. Some squadrons have rectangular fin flashes, most use the sweptback style, while two prefer it both swept and tapered! As for squadron insignia, some boldly retain it in all its glory, most use the insignia or badge in a very subdued form, and many aircraft have none at all — which is how they would all be within a matter of hours of any significant crisis or war. Individuality even extends to the serial number, which is variously painted in either white or black. Previously the RAFG attack squadrons had the serial in black on the fuselage and in large and bold white numerals on the fin!

But if the painting is apparently haphazard, the aircraft are anything but. After more than 15 years in service they are very mature, and on the whole this is probably an advantage. It cuts both ways. As the years go by, fresh problems arise; and if the structure begins to crack from fatigue this is today — thanks to inflation — likely to mean repair bills exceeding the original price of the aircraft. Fortunately the Phantom's rugged airframe is showing no sign of giving cause for major concern, and both McDonnell Aircraft and BAe Kingston-Brough Division see no reason why the FG1 and FG2 should not go on to about 1990, which is what the RAF intends. Four squadrons may even go on to 1995.

The need for substantially enhanced EW capability has been referred to earlier, and it can at least be stated that all Phantoms are intended to receive an ECM suite. In conjunction with Westinghouse, the radars are being progressively improved by the addition of new LRUs giving better functions and promising greatly extended MTBF. It is also possible that the long-range HF radio may be fitted in the FG1s, and certainly with such a long planned period of service still ahead it would make sense to bring the FG1s as far as possible up to FGR2 standard in such basic matters as the radar and communications.

Already the entire RAFG force enjoys the limited protection of HASs (hardened aircraft shelters), and similar shelters are being built for home-based Phantoms. Many of the latter are constantly at readiness in QRA (Quick-Reaction Alert) hangars, which offer more room than inside an HAS and keep the aircraft plugged in to ground power supplies and a telebrief cable, and with the crew ladder in place. In fact both men can climb aboard via the inbuilt retractable steps, but the separate ladder for the navigator saves vital seconds. At some bases, such as Leuchars, blast walls offer a degree of protection against conventional attack, but of course the Phantom, like all other aircraft tied to major airfields, is totally vulnerable to any form of nuclear missile or giant FAE (fuel/air explosive) attack.

The latter would certainly precede any major war in Europe, but fortunately nothing like this occurred in the extremely challenging Operation 'Corporate', the retaking of the Argentine-occupied Falkland Islands in the second quarter of 1982. One of the more severe problems facing the British task force was the absence of any land-based airpower, and as soon as the airfield at Port Stanley — by July 1982 called RAF Stanley — had been cleared of an incredible amount of wreckage, ammunition, mines and booby-traps, work was put in hand by the Royal Engineers, assisted by other organisations, at lengthening the 4,200ft tarmac strip, improving its battered surface and laying down a good covering of AM2 aluminium planking. Once an arrester unit had been installed and commissioned RAF Stanley was ready to receive its first-ever British airpower, other than the unique Harriers.

A detachment of 29 Squadron was assigned for an extended and indefinite period to augment the islands' defence. After an epic flight of more than 8,000 miles, with an intermediate stopover at Wideawake airfield (Ascension) and multiple air refuellings, the CO of 29 Sqn brought XV468 in to Stanley on 17 October 1983. As planned, he let the wheels touch and settle firmly and then went round again for an arrested landing. The detachment built up until it was virtually at squadron level. On 31 March 1983 it was redesignated as 23 Squadron, the original unit with that number disbanding at Wattisham. Meanwhile the original No 29 has continued as a full-status squadron at Coningsby, being augmented by Phantoms from other units.

Clearly, the need to maintain a Phantom squadron in the Falklands adds greatly to defence costs, and overall the cost of defending the islands has been estimated at £1,800million over the three years to 1985. This sum does not take into account the plan to build a new airbase with a much better 8,000ft runway, to serve as home for the Phantoms of the re-formed 23 Sqn and also strong enough for the RAF's L-1011 TriStar tanker/transports. It also leaves a gap in UK air defence, as in many other British commitments to NATO, and the White Paper published in Britain on 16 December 1982

Above:
Another view of XV418 outside an HAS at Wildenrath. In this case there are no unit markings, the serial and all stencilling is in black, and the roundels are large and B-type (two colour).
RAFG

announced that it was intended to make up the deficiency by a bargain-basement purchase of F-4J Phantoms from the US Navy or Marines. The number was at first put at 'at least 12', but this was subsequently refined to 15. Since spring 1982 a large number of surplus F-4Js have been surveyed at locations all over the United States. Five are known to have been rejected, but as this was written, in mid-1983, it was the intention to have 15 aircraft transferred to an inter-government deal and completely refurbished in the USA before being ferried to the RAF in (probably) late 1984.

They will almost certainly be designated Phantom F3, and as they will be quite unlike other RAF Phantoms they will almost certainly replace the FGR2s at present guarding the Falklands. In particular, they have J79-GE-10 engines, and there is no question of replacing these by Speys. It makes sense to keep the F3 Phantoms in a separate theatre, especially one that is if anything nearer to the American suppliers of engines and equipment than it is to the UK. Fortunately the F-4J already has a flight-refuelling probe compatible with RAF tankers, and the number of engineering change orders to be issued on these aircraft is to be held to a minimum. Thus, almost 20 years after the planners began to work on the 'British Phantom', work is now going ahead on an 'American British Phantom'.

Since this book was written, much has happened to the RAF Phantom programme. In particular, and inexplicably, the documents at MoD on the F-4J continue to use the US designation, even though changing to the British style as F3 is almost the only thing in modern defence that would not cost a penny. Despite the apparent sense in sending the RAF's F-4Js — the 15 of which are priced at an initial £124.9million — to re-equip 23 Sqn in the Falklands, they are, in fact, assigned to 74 Sqn, which is being re-formed at RAF Wattisham. It will be recalled that this unit, 'the Tigers', was the first to receive the Lightning F1 in 1959-60. Meanwhile, though the 23 Sqn FGR2s stay 8,000 miles away, their crews are replaced in rotation from Phantom crews in Europe.

Another new move is a 1984 contract with Ferranti for two CEPT (cockpit emergency procedure trainer) simulators, one representing the FGR.2 (and actually using a crashed fuselage) and the other the F-4J (and, despite the profusion of available airframes, built by Ferranti from scratch). Each is mounted in a large trailer so that it can be driven to different Phantom airfields for use while the main mission simulator is being refurbished. There is no attempt at external visual system or cockpit motion, but with BAe data the instruments are driven by computers to respond correctly during each simulated mission, while an instructor injects any desired emergency. Both CEPTs will be delivered in 1985, 20 years after the RAF Phantoms were ordered.

RESCUE
K

Above left:
Another UK-based Phantom, aircraft 'W' of 23 Sqn (since disbanded), scrambles at Wattisham in March 1982. Stencilling is white and roundels are B-type but small. *MoD(RAF)*

Left:
Aircraft 'K' of 56 Squadron waits fully armed in the QRA hangar at Wattisham on 9 March 1982. In this case the squadron insignia, though reduced in size, is painted in its original high-contrast colours, including the checkerboard on the ECM fin cap. *MoD(RAF)*

Above:
After one of the longest (and, with no alternates, most challenging) of all Phantom deployments, the CO of 29 Sqn, Wg Cdr Ian Macfadyen and navigator Sqn Ldr Peter Simpson make a touch-and-go on the runway at RAF Stanley, Falkland Islands. They made a quick circuit and then an arrested landing. *MoD(RAF)*

Right:
Having at last vacated XV468 Wg Cdr Macfadyen is warmly welcomed by Maj-Gen David Thorne, Falklands Commander, Land Forces. *MoD(RAF)*

Above:
Another photograph of 'W' of 23 Sqn, this time with the 500gal centreline tank and braking parachute deployed. *23 Sqn*

Below:
Ready for practice interception, Phantom 'X' of 23 Sqn is parked at Wattisham with an STM under each wing and the telebrief lead plugged in. *23 Sqn*

APPENDICES

1
BASIC SPECIFICATIONS

Designation: F-4K (Phantom FG1), F-4M (Phantom FGR2), F-4J mod (Phantom F3)
Engines: (FG1) two Rolls-Royce Spey 203 augmented turbofans each with maximum rating of 20,515lb (reheat) or 12,250lb (dry); (FGR2) two Spey 202, same ratings; (F3) two General Electric J79-8B or -10 afterburning turbojets each rated at 17,900lb (reheat) or 11,810lb (dry)
Dimensions: Span 38ft 5in; length (FG1, FGR2) 57ft 7in (F3), 58ft $3\frac{3}{4}$in; height (with ARI18228) 16ft 9in; wing area 530sq ft
Weights: Empty (FG1) typically 31,000lb, (FGR2) 31,350lb, (3) 29,900lb; max (all, in UK service, 7.75g below Mach 1) 58,000lb
Performance: Max level speed (FG1, FGR2) 1,386mph (Mach 2.1) at 40,000ft, (F3) 1,434mph (Mach 2.17) at 40,000ft; initial climb (FG1, FGR2) 32,000ft/min, (F3) 41,750ft/min; service ceiling (FG1, FGR2) 57,200ft, (F3) 61,900ft

Below:
A future Phantom F3 (this designation is speculative) is BuAer No 153785, seen here landing at MCAS Kaneohe Bay, Hawaii, in March 1969. Unit markings have been painted out because 3785 was returning from Vietnam for fresh assignment. Later she served with VMFA-232 'Red Devils' at MCAS Iwakuni, Japan. *USMC via R. F. Dorr*

2
AIRCRAFT BUILT

F-4K programme
2 YF-4K prototypes (MAC Nos 1449, 1527; British serials XT595/6); 2 pre-production F-4K (MAC 1611, 1669; XT597/8); 48 production (XT857/876, XV565/592). Total 52. First delivery 25 April 1968; last aircraft completed 29 July 1969 and delivered early August.

F-4M programme
2 YF-4M prototypes (MAC 1950, 2020; XT852/3); 116 production (from MAC 2250, XT891/914, XV393/442, XV460/501). Total 118. Total UK buy 170. First delivery from St Louis 23 August 1968; last delivery 29 August 1969.

F-4J (F3) purchase
The following record has been assembled by Robert F. Dorr concerning the secondhand F-4J Phantoms which are now to equip No 74 Squadron RAF: they are USN BuAer Nos 153768, 153773, 153783, 153785, 153795, 153803, 153850, 153892, 155510, 155529, 155574, 155734, 155755, 155868, 155894 and the RAF serials will be, in sequence, ZE350-ZE364.

US Navy fighter squadron VF-102 traditionally operated on the East Coast and with the Atlantic fleet, but this picture was taken in about 1973 of an air refuelling from a KA-6D of VA-65 over California. By 1979 the nearer F-4J, 155510, was with VF-103 at NAS Oceana. Today she is being refurbished for further service as an RAF fighter. *R. F. Dorr*

498